A DOZEN ANTHOLOGY

by Edna Mae Burnam

Includes Online Audio
Orchestrations by Ric Ianonne

PLAYBACK+
Speed • Pitch • Balance • Loop

The exclusive **PLAYBACK+** feature allows tempo changes without altering the pitch.
Loop points can also be set for repetition of tricky measures.

To access audio, visit:
www.halleonard.com/mylibrary

Enter Code
7608-3152-4808-1635

ISBN 978-1-4950-6116-5

WILLIS MUSIC

EXCLUSIVELY DISTRIBUTED BY

HAL•LEONARD®

Visit Hal Leonard Online at
www.halleonard.com

Contact us:
Hal Leonard
7777 West Bluemound Road
Milwaukee, WI 53213
Email: info@halleonard.com

In Europe, contact:
Hal Leonard Europe Limited
42 Wigmore Street
Marylebone, London, W1U 2RN
Email: info@halleonardeurope.com

In Australia, contact:
Hal Leonard Australia Pty. Ltd.
4 Lentara Court
Cheltenham, Victoria, 3192 Australia
Email: info@halleonard.com.au

"Edna Mae Burnam was a pioneer in the piano pedagogy publishing field. I was privileged to work with her for many years, and she was an absolute delight. Every time we talked I left feeling upbeat and happy, and she had that effect on everyone she met. Edna Mae had the most wonderful outlook on life and delighted in helping people learn to make music."

Kevin Cranley
President, Willis Music

PREFACE

Many people do exercises every morning before they go to work.

Likewise, we should give our fingers exercises every day before we begin our practicing.

The purpose of this book is to help develop strong hands and flexible fingers.

Do not try to learn the entire first dozen exercises the first week you study this book! Learn two or three exercises, and do them each day before practicing. When these are mastered, add another, then another, and keep adding until the twelve exercises can be played perfectly.

When the first dozen—or Group I—has been mastered and perfected, Group II may be introduced in the same manner, and so on for the other Groups.

Many of these exercises may be transposed to different keys. In fact, this should be encouraged.

EDNA MAE BURNAM

A DOZEN A DAY
MINI BOOK

A DOZEN A DAY
PREPARATORY BOOK

A DOZEN A DAY
BOOK 1

A DOZEN A DAY
BOOK 2

A DOZEN A DAY

Technical Exercises
FOR THE PIANO
to be done each day
BEFORE *practicing*

by

Edna Mae Burnam

EXCLUSIVELY DISTRIBUTED BY

 WILLIS MUSIC

 HAL•LEONARD®
CORPORATION
7777 W. BLUEMOUND RD. P.O. BOX 13819
MILWAUKEE, WISCONSIN 53213

Visit Hal Leonard Online at
www.halleonard.com

To my family

Group I

1. Walking

2. Hopping

3. Bouncing A Ball With Right Hand

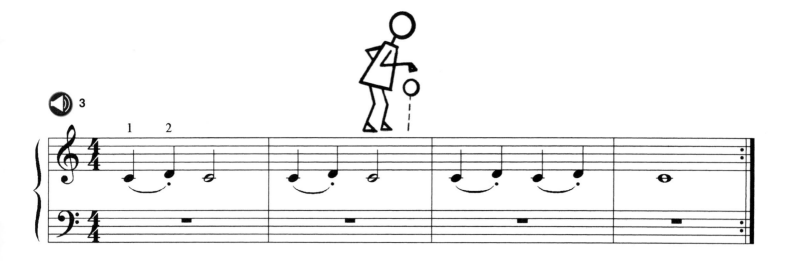

4. Bouncing A Ball With Left Hand

5. Rolling

6. Arms Up And Down

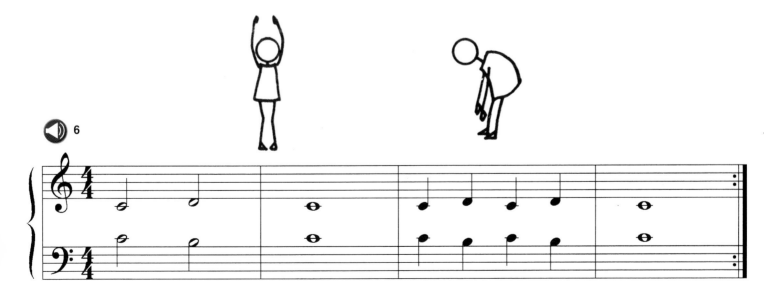

7. Skipping

8. Deep Breathing

9. Hammering With Right Hand

Set thumb down silent.
Hold down throughout exercise.

10. Hammering With Left Hand

Set thumb down silent.
Hold down throughout exercise.

11. Walking In A Water Puddle In Boots

12. Fit As A Fiddle And Ready To Go

Now my fin-gers feel so good. I can play the way I should.

Group II

1. Twisting Right And Left

13

2. Flinging Arms Out And Back

14

3. Touching Toes

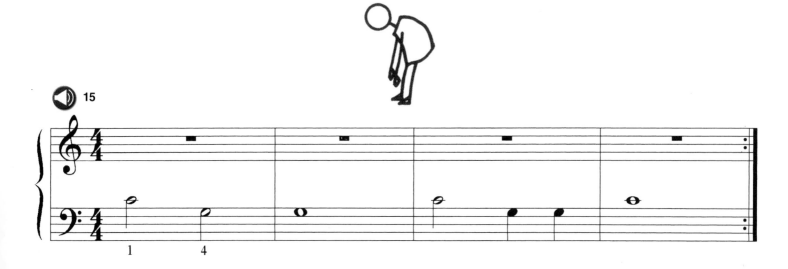

15

4. Kicking Right Leg Up

5. Kicking Left Leg Up

6. Backward Bend

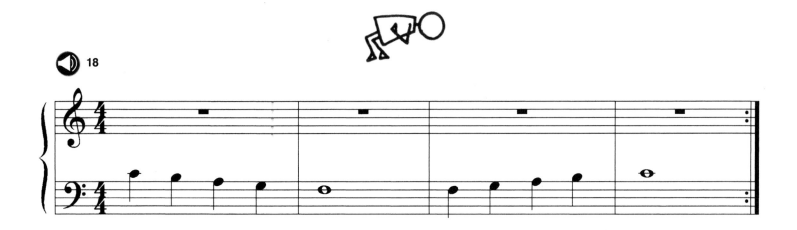

7. Stretching Legs Out And Back (sitting down)

8. Skipping

9. Deep Breathing

10. Jump Rope

11. Walking Down A Hill

12. Fit As A Fiddle And Ready To Go

Now I'm nim - ble as can be. I can play this mel - o - dy.

Group III

1. The Splits

2. Deep Breathing

3. Wide Walk (Stiff-Legged)

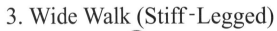

4. Right Knee Up And Back (Lying Down)

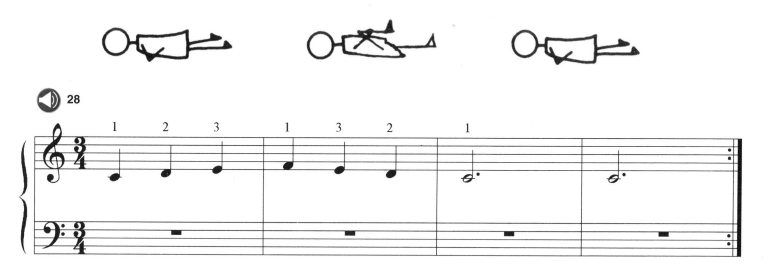

5. Left Knee Up And Back (Lying Down)

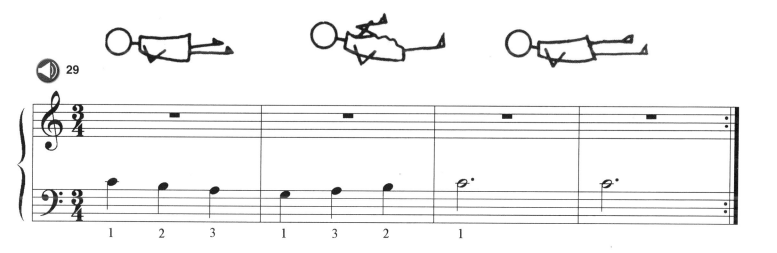

6. Both Knees Up And Back (Lying Down)

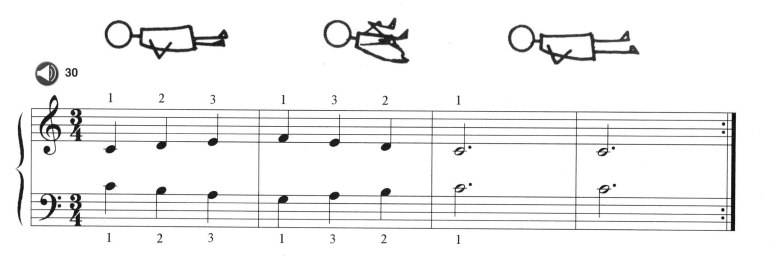

7. Backward Bend

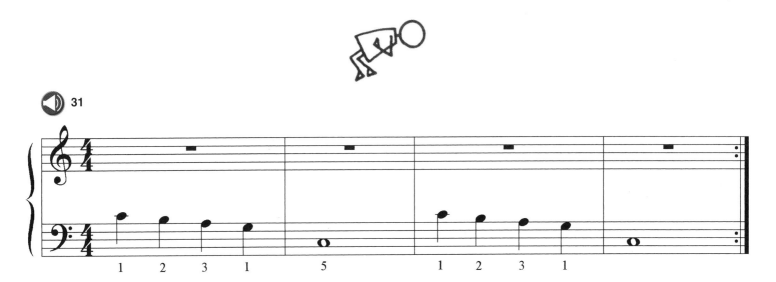

8. Twirling To The Right

9. Twirling To The Left

21

10. Jumping Over A Bench

11. Jumping Off A Big Box

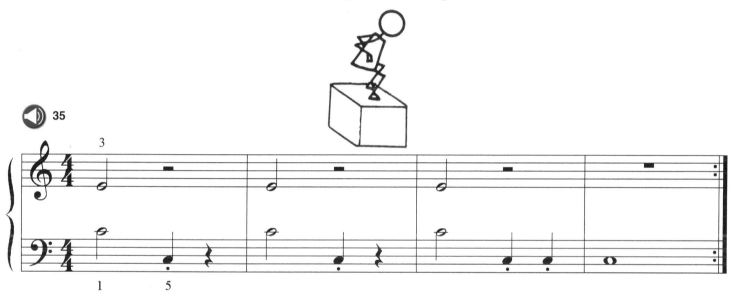

12. Fit As A Fiddle And Ready To Go

Read - y to go, Play - ing mu - sic I know.

Group IV

1. Walking On A Sunny Day

2. Walking On A Cloudy Day

3. Skipping On A Sunny Day

4. Skipping On a Cloudy Day

40

5. Deep Breathing On A Sunny Day

41

6. Deep Breathing On A Cloudy Day

42

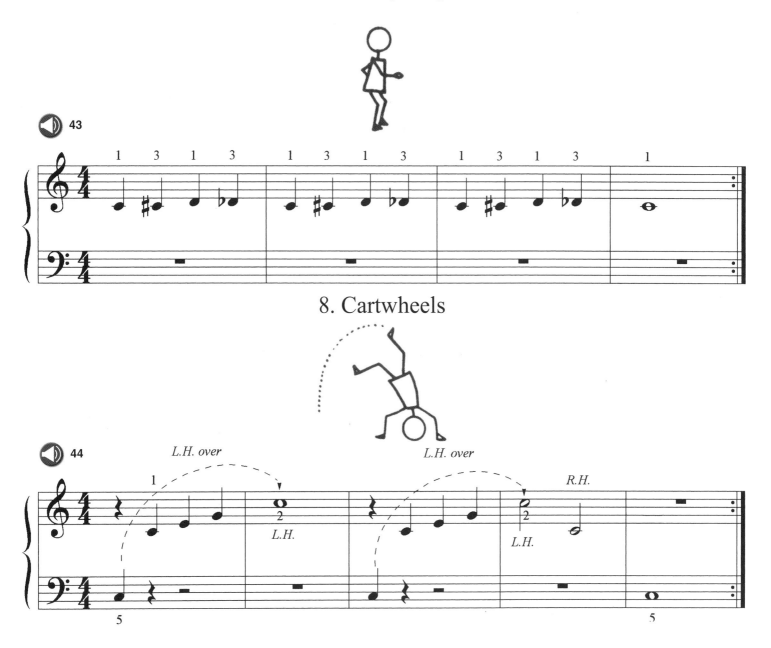

7. Baby Steps

8. Cartwheels

9. Leap Frog

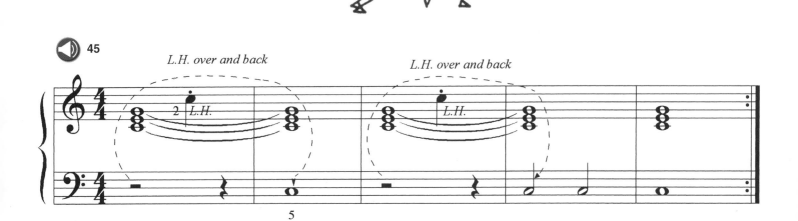

10. Tightrope Walking

🔊 46

Silent change.
Keep key down while
changing fingers.

11. Walking On Tiptoes

🔊 47

12. Fit As A Fiddle And Ready To Go

🔊 48

Fin - gers read - y   as can be.   Play - ing mu - sic   just for me.

Group V

1. Running

2. In A Swing

3. Teeter-Totter

4. Whirly Gig Ride

52

5. Swimming

53

6. Going Down A Slide

54

7. Climbing Monkey Bars

8. Hanging By Knees On Acting Bar

Hold Middle C down
while playing other notes in measure.

9. Walking On Trapeze Rings

10. Jump Rope

11. Tether Ball

12. Fit As A Fiddle And Ready To Go

Nim - ble, nim - ble fin - gers   like   to   play   Lots of nim - ble notes to - day.____

PREPARATORY BOOK

A DOZEN A DAY

Technical Exercises
FOR THE PIANO
to be done each day
BEFORE *practicing*

by

Edna Mae Burnam

EXCLUSIVELY DISTRIBUTED BY

WILLIS MUSIC

HAL•LEONARD®
CORPORATION
7777 W. BLUEMOUND RD. P.O. BOX 13819
MILWAUKEE, WISCONSIN 53213

Visit Hal Leonard Online at
www.halleonard.com

To Chris and Billy

Group I

1. Walking

2. Running

3. Skipping

4. Jumping

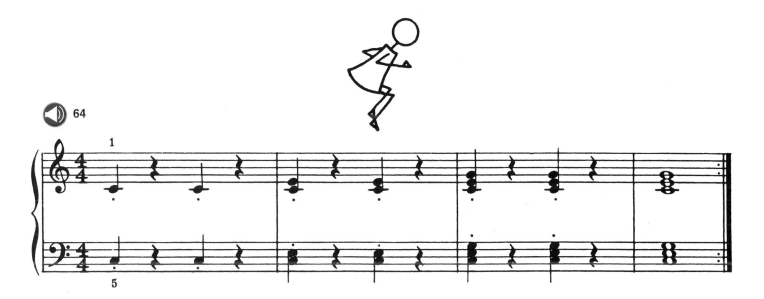

5. The Splits

6. Deep Breathing

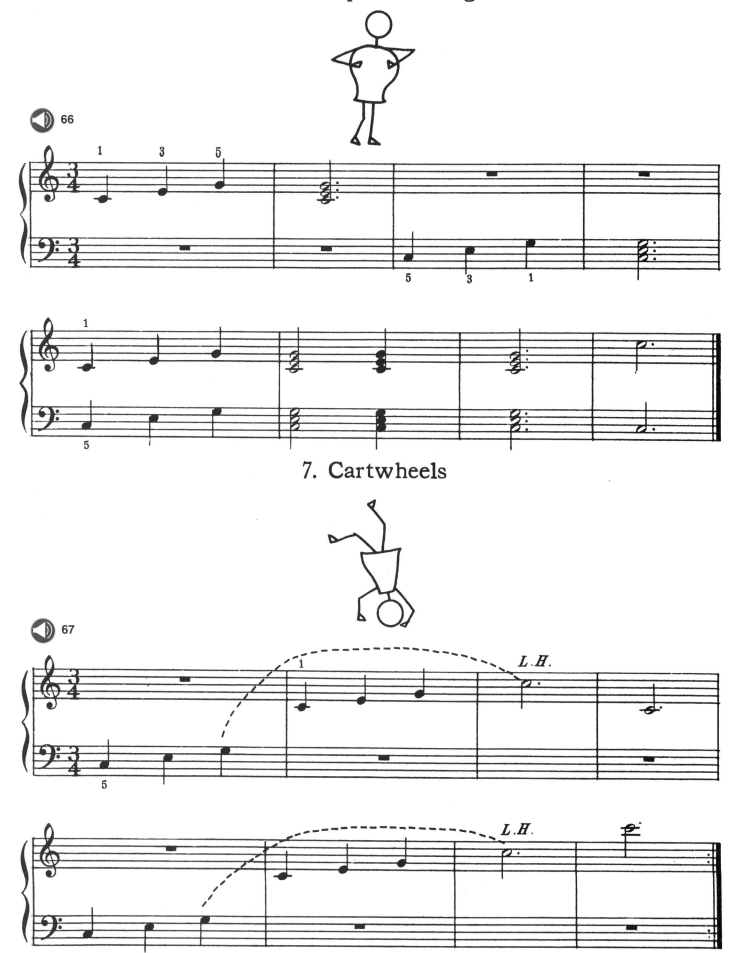

7. Cartwheels

8. Deep Knee Bend

9. Hopping On Right Foot

10. Hopping On Left Foot

11. Standing On Head

12. Fit As A Fiddle and Ready To Go

Group II

1. Stretching

2. Tiptoe Running

3. Jumping Off The Front Porch Steps

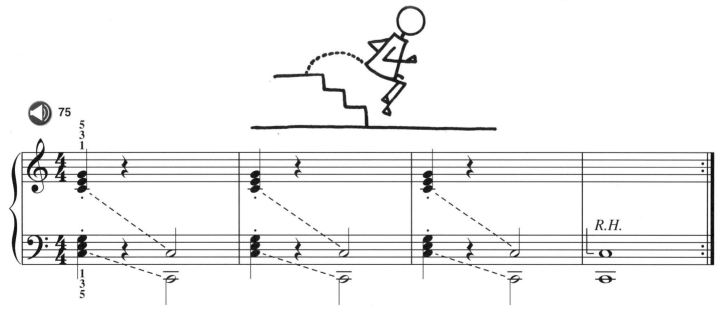

4. Climbing Up A Ladder

5. Going Down A Ladder

6. Jumping Like A Frog

7. Hanging From Bar by Right Hand

11. Swinging

83

12. Fit As A Fiddle and Ready To Go

84

Fit as a fid - dle, All day long;

Ex - er - cise will make my fin - gers ver - y strong.

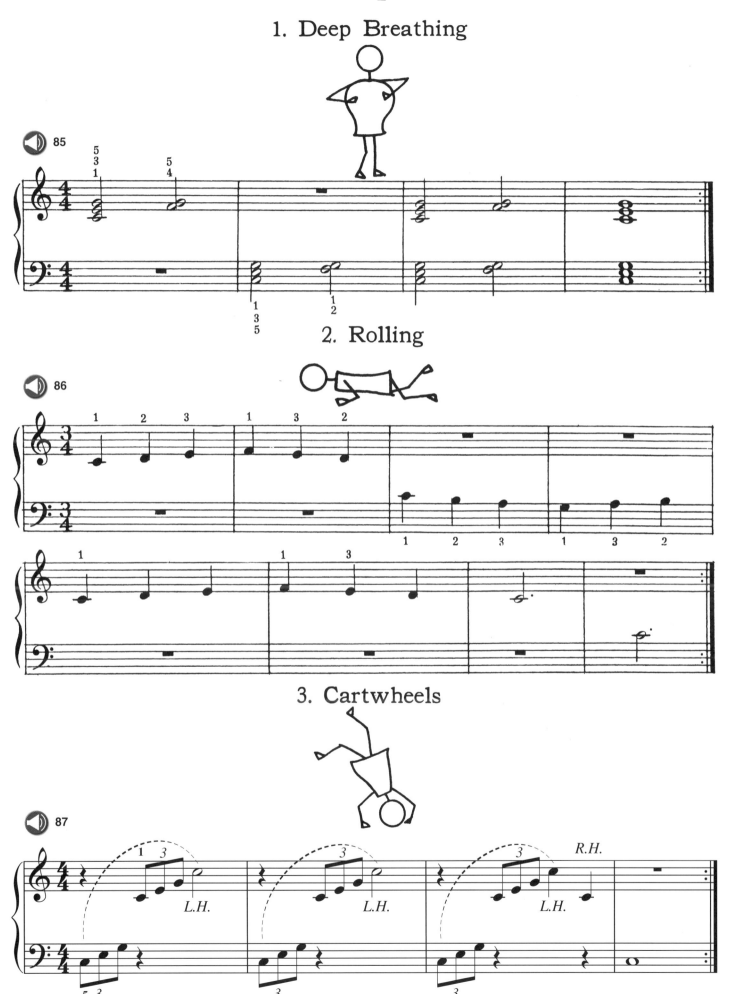

4. Skipping

5. Jumping Rope (Slow, and "Red Pepper")

6. Rocking

🔊 90

7. Round And Round In A Swing

🔊 91

Winding

Slow

Unwinding

Faster

44

8. Jump The River

92

9. Climbing

93

10. Ping Pong

94

11. Sitting Up and Lying Down

12. Fit As A Fiddle and Ready To Go

Fit as a fid - dle, Ex - er - cise my fin - gers ev - 'ry day;

Fit as a fid - dle, Ex - er - cise will make my fin - gers play.

Group IV

1. Deep Breathing

2. Walking On A Sunny, Then A Cloudy Day

Sunny day

Cloudy day

3. Skipping On A Sunny, Then A Cloudy Day

99

Sunny day

Cloudy day

4. Cartwheels On A Sunny, Then A Cloudy Day

100

Sunny day

Cloudy day

L.H.

5. Jumping On A Sunny, Then A Cloudy Day

6. Running On A Sunny, Then A Cloudy Day

7. Walking Pigeon-toed

8. Wiggling Toes

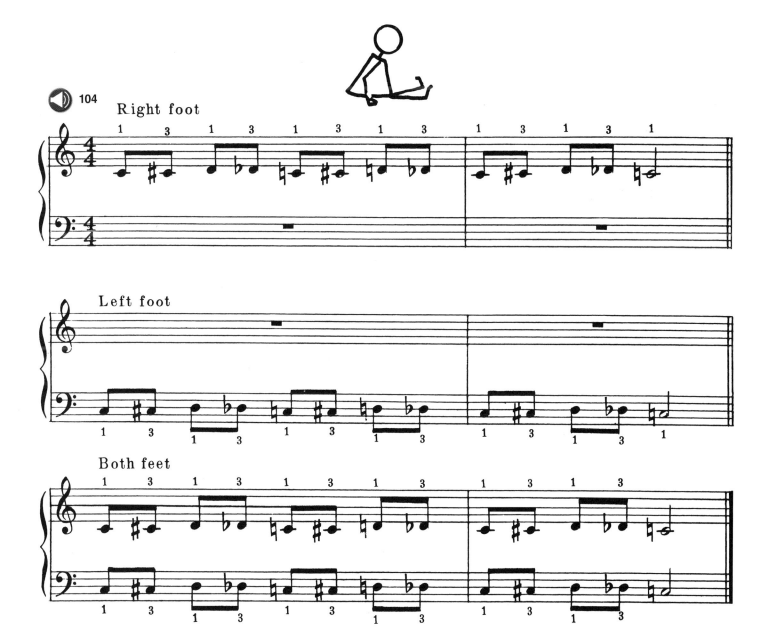

9. Teeter-Totter

10. Peeking Between Knees

11. Bouncing A Ball

12. Fit As A Fiddle and Ready To Go

If I do my Doz-en A___ Day, From top to toe and the mid - dle,

Then I know I'll al - ways___ stay Just as fit as a fid - dle.

Group V

1. Walking Up A Hill

2. Taking Deep Breaths
While Walking Up A Hill

3. Running Up A Hill

4. Skipping Up A Hill

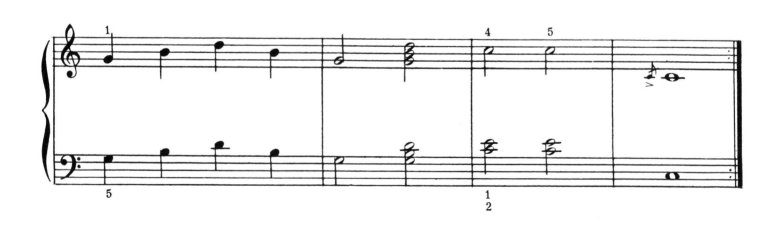

5. Cartwheels Up A Hill

6. Jumping Up A Hill

7. Boxing

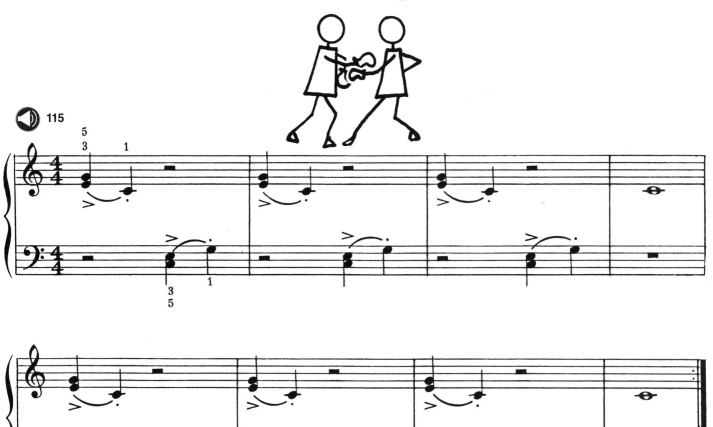

8. Spinning A Big Top

9. Rolling A Hoop

10. Raising Arms Up and Up On Toes

11. Riding Piggyback

12. Fit As A Fiddle and Ready To Go

NOTES or REMINDERS

(Or, draw your own stick figure!)

BOOK ONE

A DOZEN A DAY

Technical Exercises
FOR THE PIANO
to be done each day
BEFORE practicing

by

Edna Mae Burnam

WILLIS MUSIC

EXCLUSIVELY DISTRIBUTED BY

HAL•LEONARD®
CORPORATION
7777 W. BLUEMOUND RD. P.O. BOX 13819
MILWAUKEE, WISCONSIN 53213

Visit Hal Leonard Online at
www.halleonard.com

Group I

1. Walking and Running

121

1st time—legato (smooth, connected)
2nd time—staccato (sharp, detached)

2. Skipping

122

legato—staccato

3. Hopping

123

staccato

4. Deep Breathing

124

5. Deep Knee Bend

125

6. Stretching

126

L.H.

7. Stretching Right Leg Up

8. Stretching Left Leg

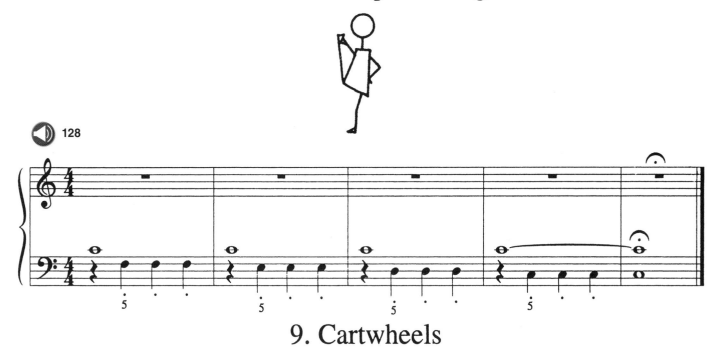

9. Cartwheels

10. The Splits

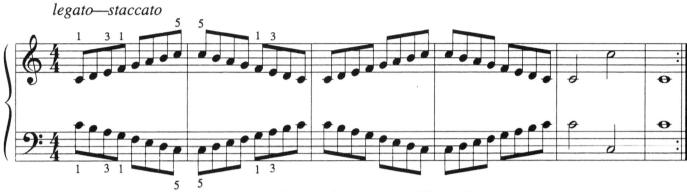

11. Standing on Head

12. Fit as a Fiddle and Ready To Go

Group II
1. Morning Stretch

133

2. Walking

134

legato—staccato

3. Running

135

legato—staccato

7. Kicking Left Leg

139

8. The Splits

140

9. Leg Work (lying down)

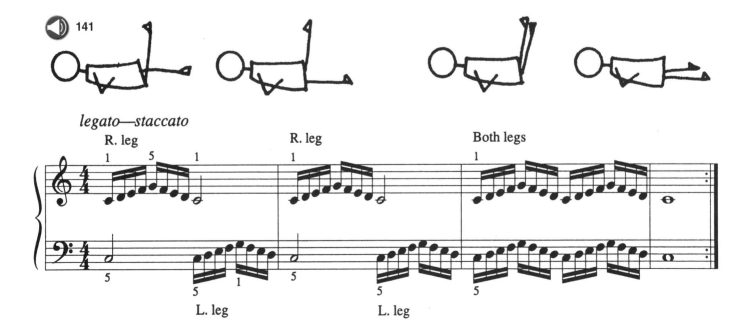

141

legato—staccato

R. leg   R. leg   Both legs

L. leg   L. leg

10. Sitting Up and Lying Down

legato—staccato

11. A Hard Trick

143

Practice this first:

Then practice this:

legato—staccato   *legato—staccato*

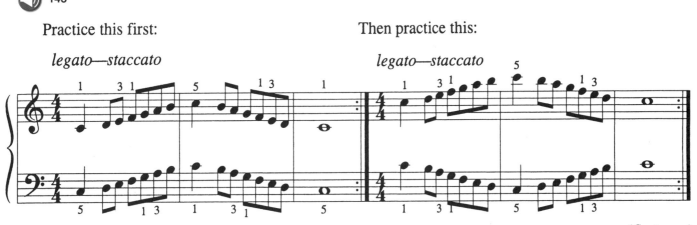

(Cont. over)

Now do the whole trick:

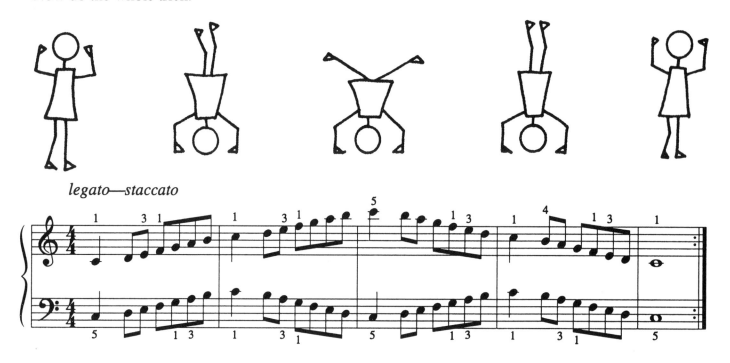

legato—staccato

12. Fit as a Fiddle and Ready To Go

Group III
1. Deep Breathing

145

2. Rolling

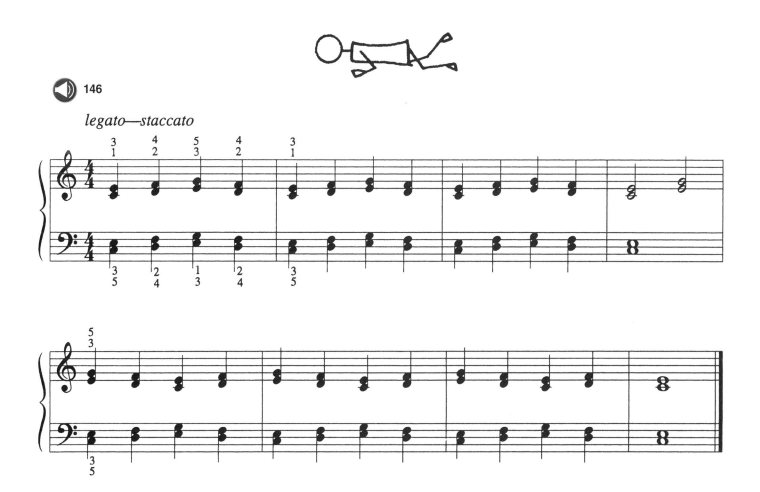

146

legato—staccato

3. Climbing (in place)

147

legato—staccato

4. Tiptoe Running (in place)

148

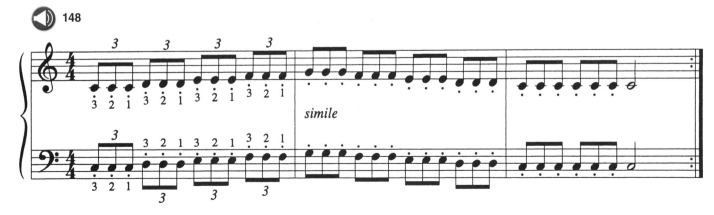

5. Baby Steps

149

legato—staccato

6. Giant Steps

150

7. Jumping Rope

151

8. Somersaults

9. Touching Toes

10. Ballet Exercise ("Entre chat quatre")

11. The Splits

12. Fit as a Fiddle and Ready To Go

Group IV

1. Morning Stretch

2. Climbing (in place)

legato—staccato

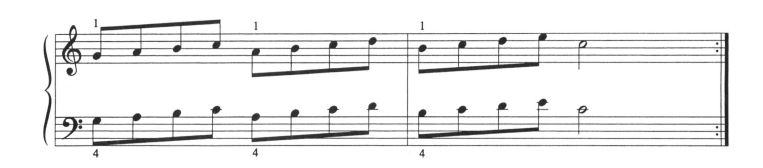

3. Tiptoe Running (in place)

159

4. Running

160

legato—staccato

5. Cartwheels

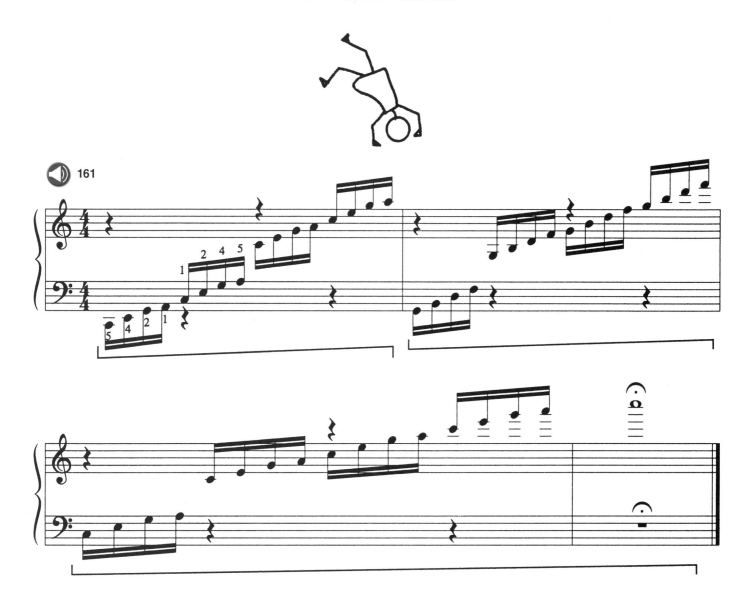

6. Touching Toes

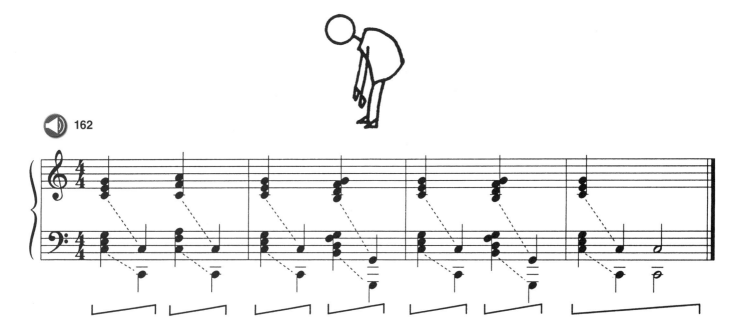

7. Hopping

8. Baby Steps

legato—staccato

9. Giant Steps

10. Flinging Arms Out and Back

11. Standing on Head

12. Fit as a Fiddle and Ready To Go

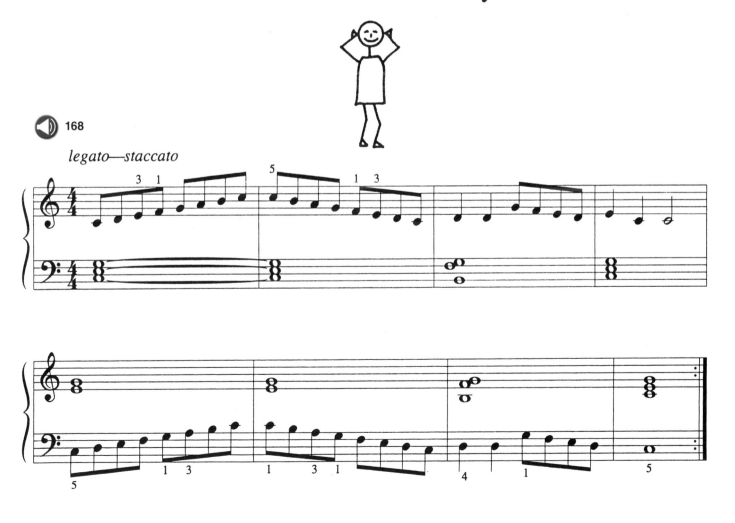

Group V
1. Deep Breathing

2. Touching Toes

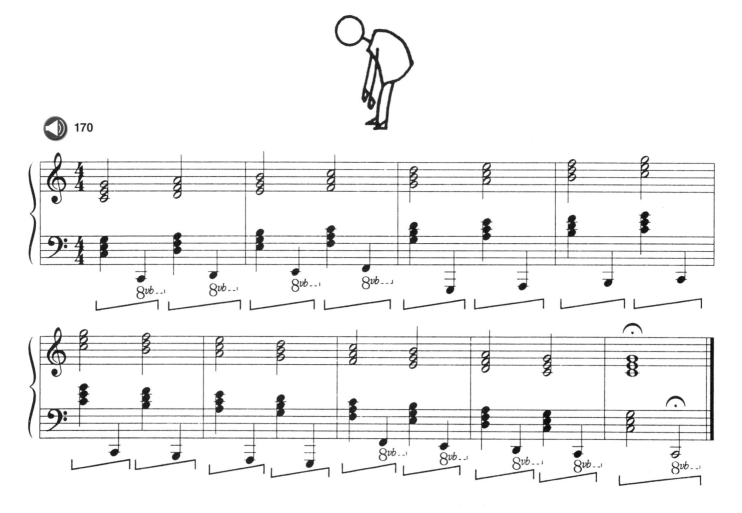

3. Hopping

4. Climbing a Ladder

5. Jumping Rope (Slow, and "Red Pepper")

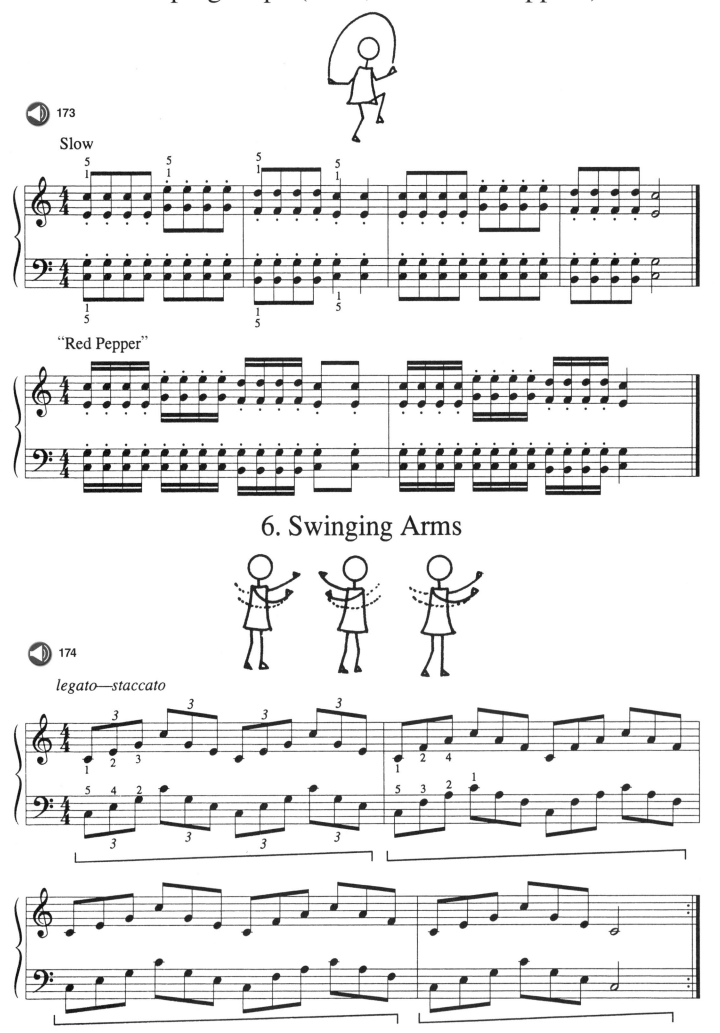

7. Hand Springs

8. Walking Like a Duck

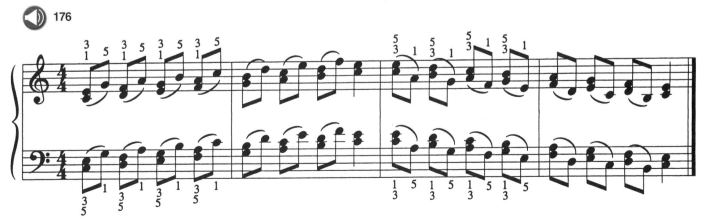

9. Bear Walk

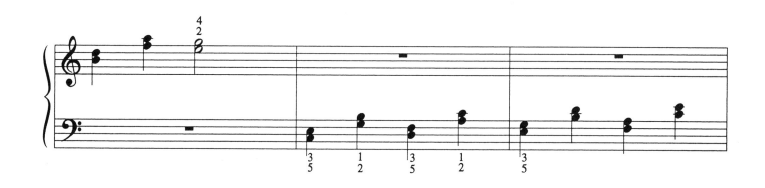

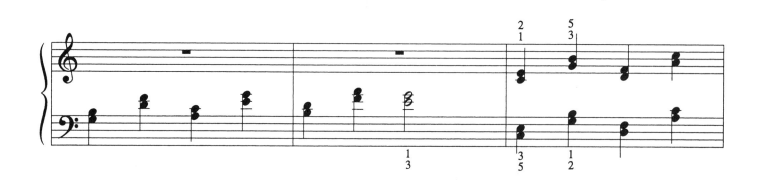

10. Sliding Down the Bannister

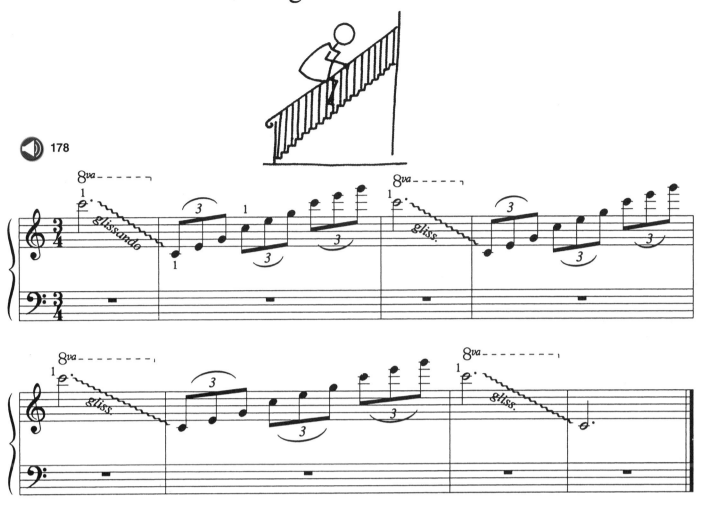

178

11. A Hard Trick

179

Practice this first:

legato—staccato

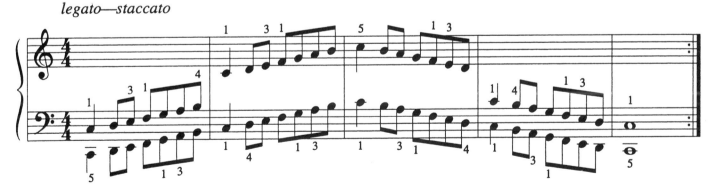

Now practice this:

legato—staccato

(Cont. over)

Now do the whole trick:

legato—staccato

12. Fit as a Fiddle and Ready To Go

BOOK TWO

A DOZEN A DAY

Technical Exercises
FOR THE PIANO
to be done each day
BEFORE practicing

by

Edna Mae Burnam

WILLIS MUSIC

EXCLUSIVELY DISTRIBUTED BY

HAL•LEONARD®
CORPORATION
7777 W. BLUEMOUND RD. P.O. BOX 13819
MILWAUKEE, WISCONSIN 53213

Visit Hal Leonard Online at
www.halleonard.com

Group I

1. Wake Up and Stretch

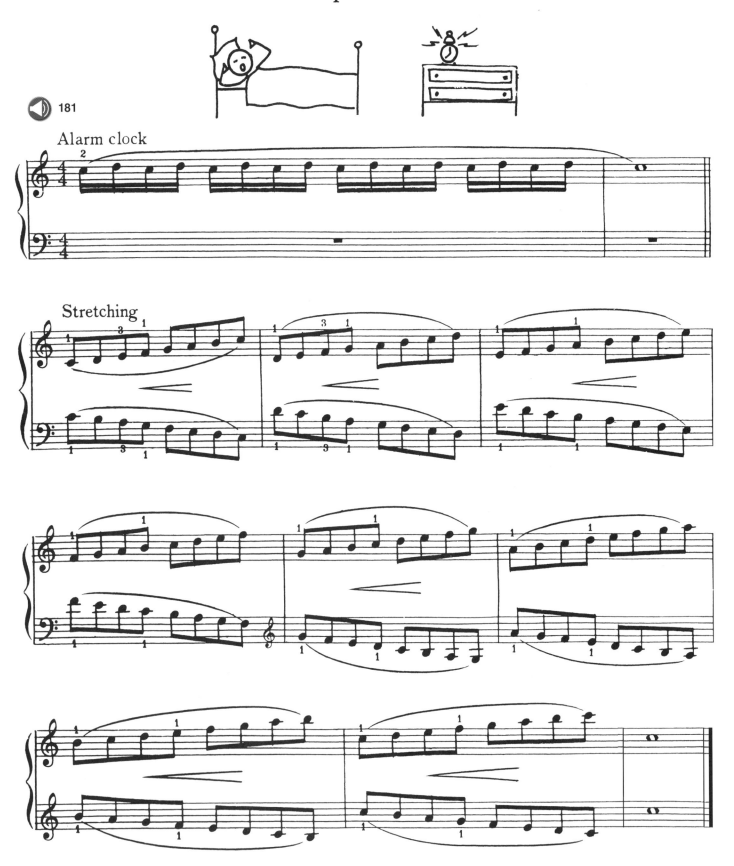

2. Brushing Teeth

3. Going Down Stairs

4. Chinning Yourself

5. Walking

6. Running

7. Jumping

8. Backward Bend

9. Flinging Arms Out and Back

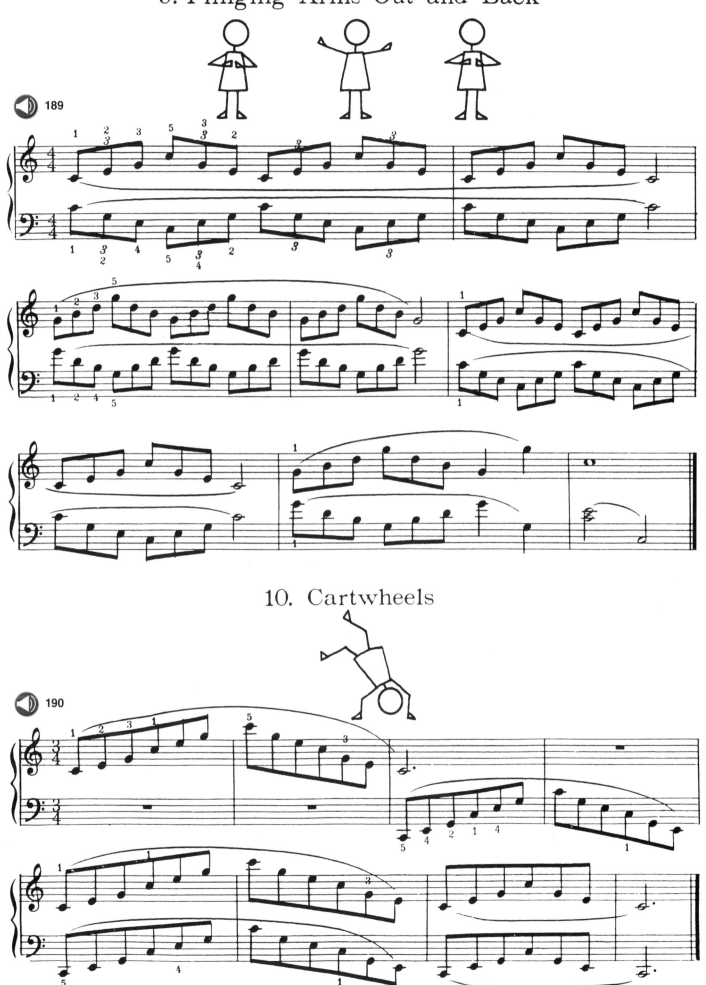

10. Cartwheels

11. The Push-Up

12. Fit as a Fiddle and Ready To Go

Group II

1. Deep Breathing

2. Brushing Teeth

3. The Broad Jump

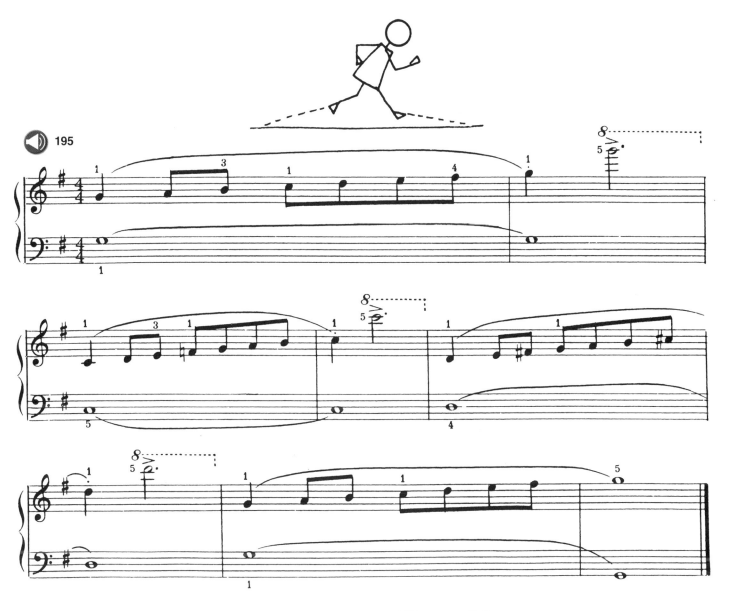

4. Chinning Yourself

5. Climbing (in place)

197

6. The Splits

198

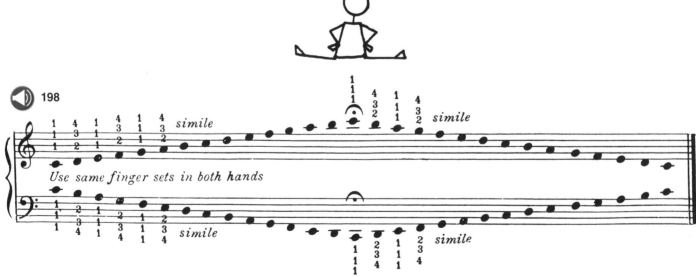

7. O-Leary

One, two, three O-Lear-y | Four, five, six O-Lear-y

Seven, eight, nine O-Lear-y | Ten, eleven, twelve O-Lear-y. | One O-Lear-y two O-Lear-y

three O-Lear-y four. | I would like to do O-Lear-y | for for-ev-er-more.

8. Leap Frog

9. Jump The River

10. Whirling

11. Going Up Stairs

12. Fit as a Fiddle and Ready To Go

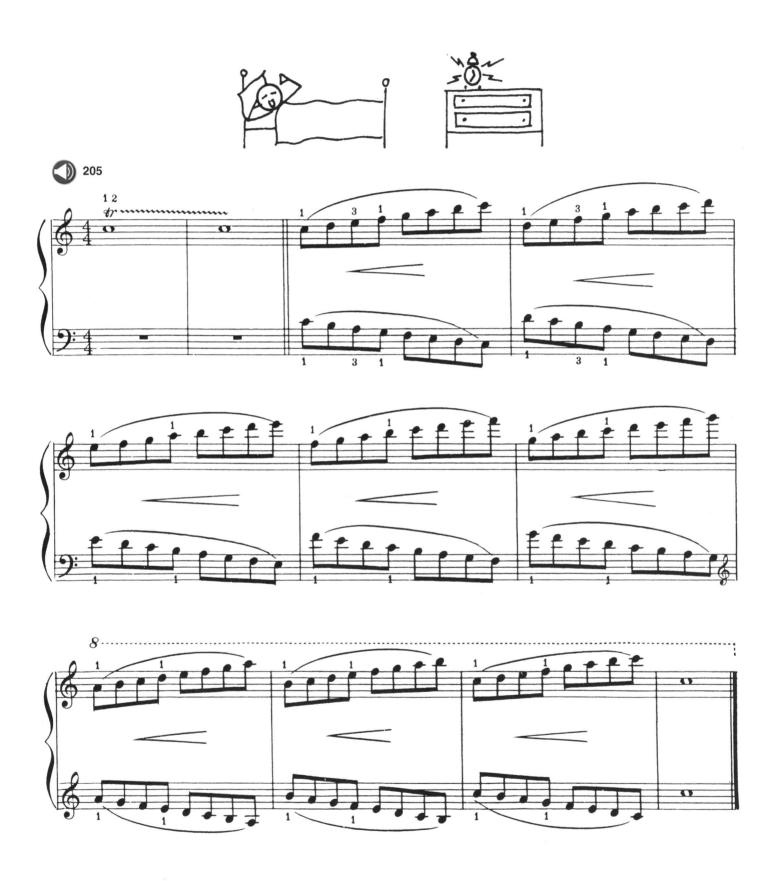

106

Group III

1. Wake Up and Stretch

205

2. Deep Breathing

3. Jumping Feet Apart and Flinging Arms Out

4. Crossing Leg Over (lying down)

208

Left leg over

Right leg over

5. Chinning Yourself

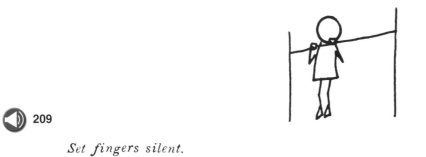

209

Set fingers silent.
Hold down throughout exercise.

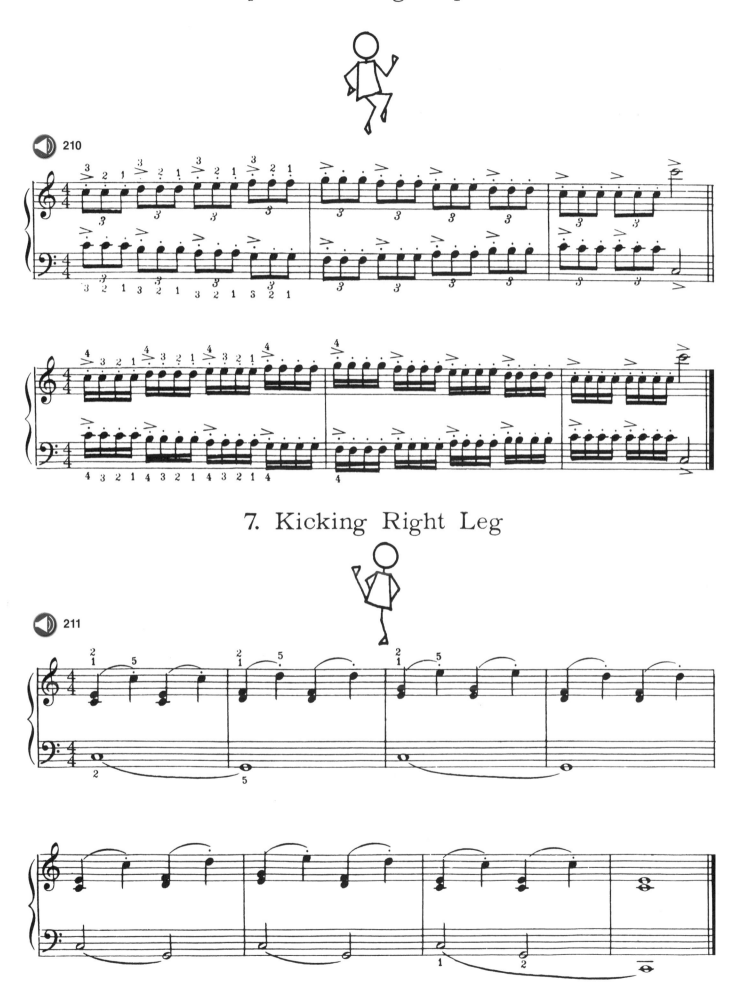

6. Tiptoe Running (in place)

7. Kicking Right Leg

8. Kicking Left Leg

9. Jumping Like A Frog (both feet at once)

10. Running

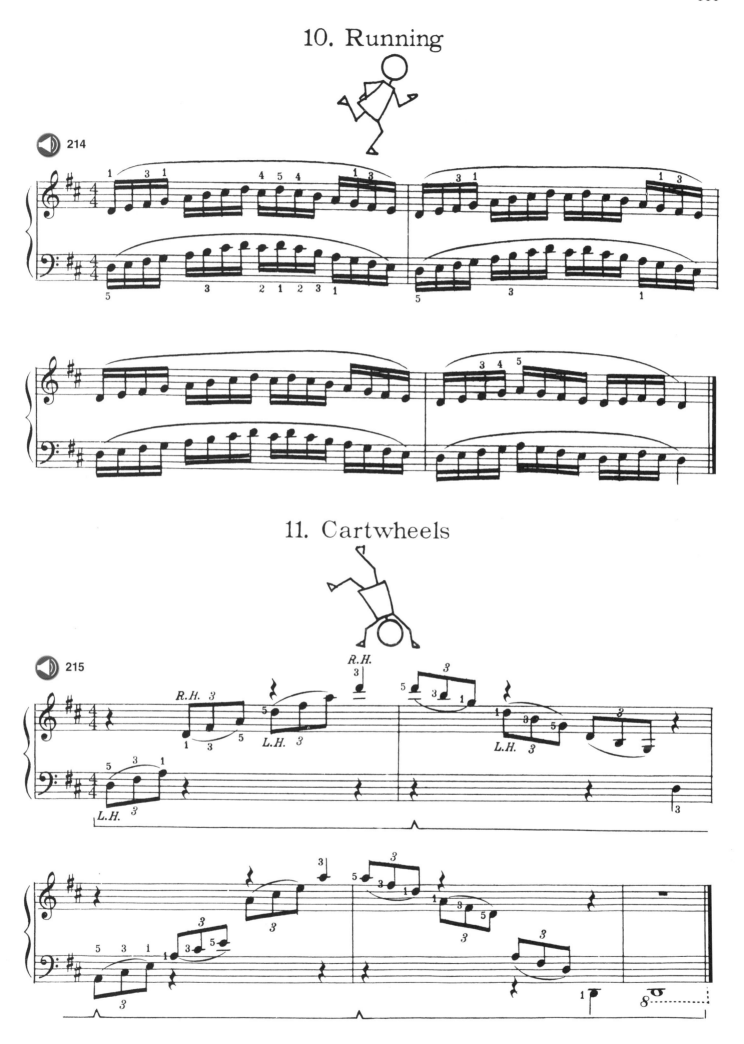

11. Cartwheels

12. Fit as a Fiddle and Ready To Go

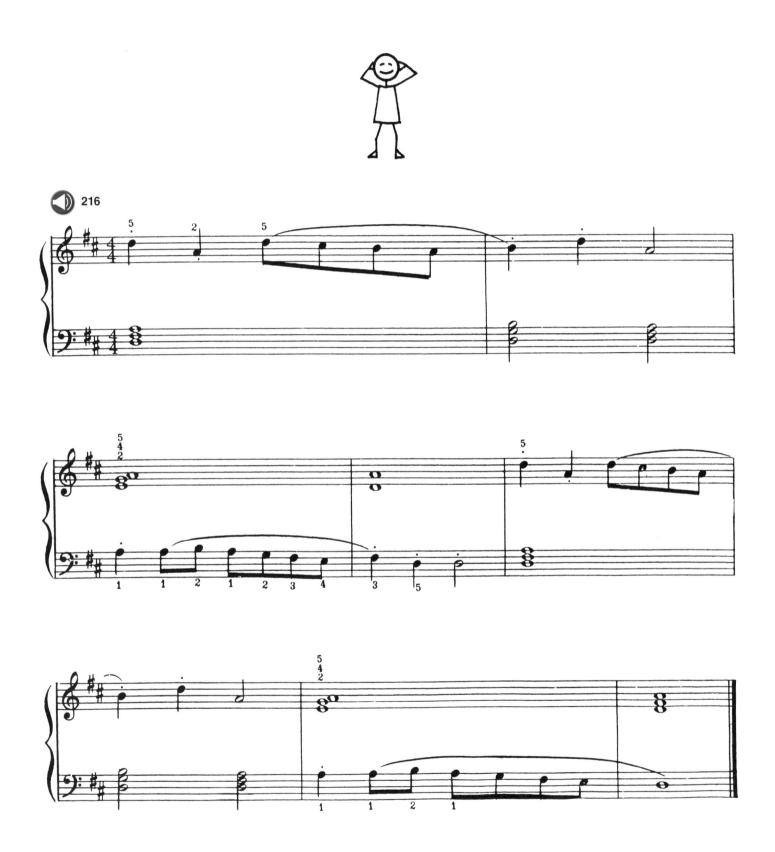

Group IV

1. Deep Breathing

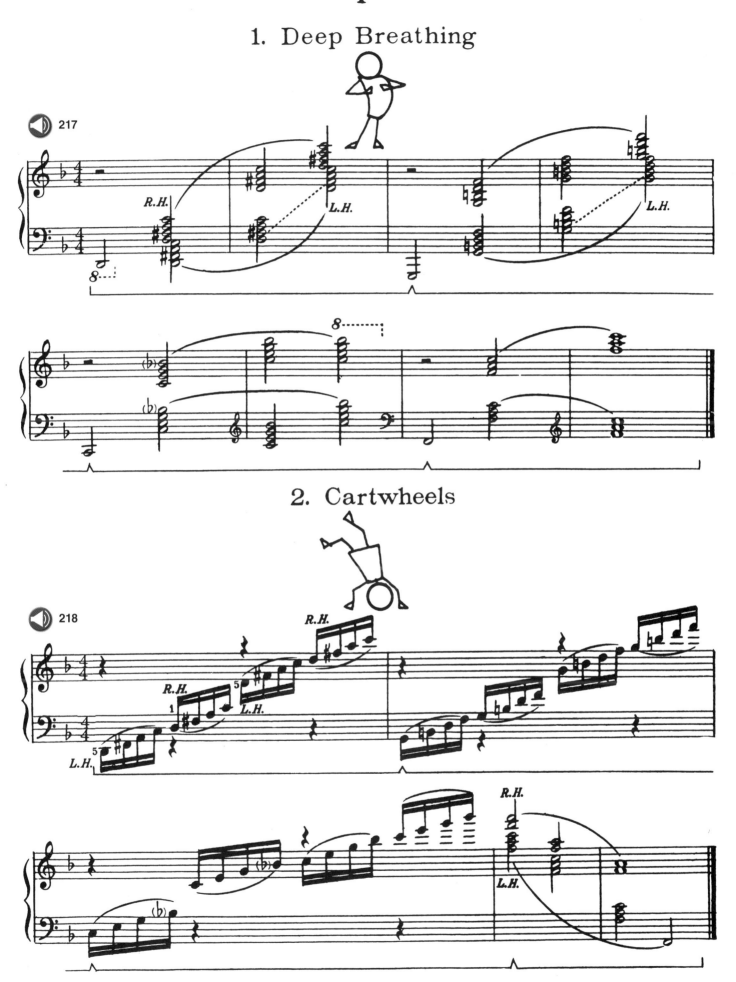

2. Cartwheels

3. Walking On Stilts

4. Walking a Tightrope

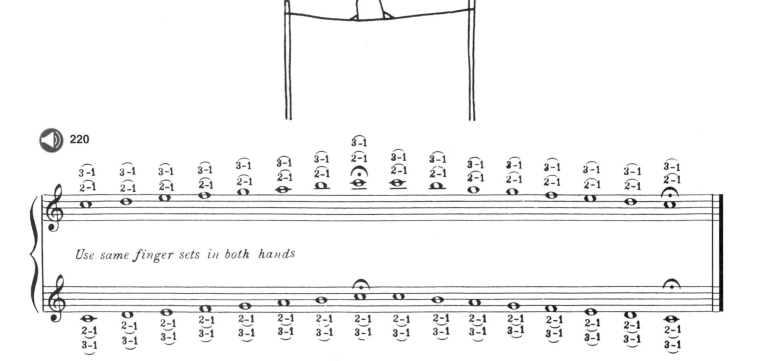

Use same finger sets in both hands

5. Chinning Yourself

6. Going Up and Down a Rope

7. Skipping

8. Running

9. Turning Right Leg Around In a Circle

10. Turning Left Leg Around In a Circle

11. Hanging By Your Knees

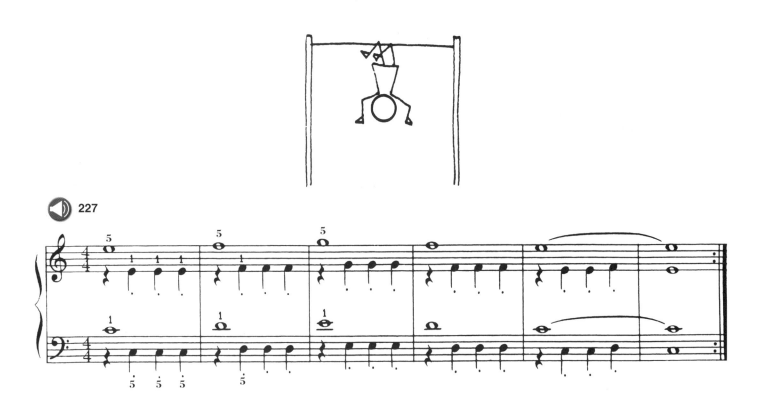

12. Fit as a Fiddle and Ready To Go

Group V

1. Deep Breathing

2. Sliding Down A Pole (a little bit at a time)

3. Chinning Yourself

4. Cartwheels

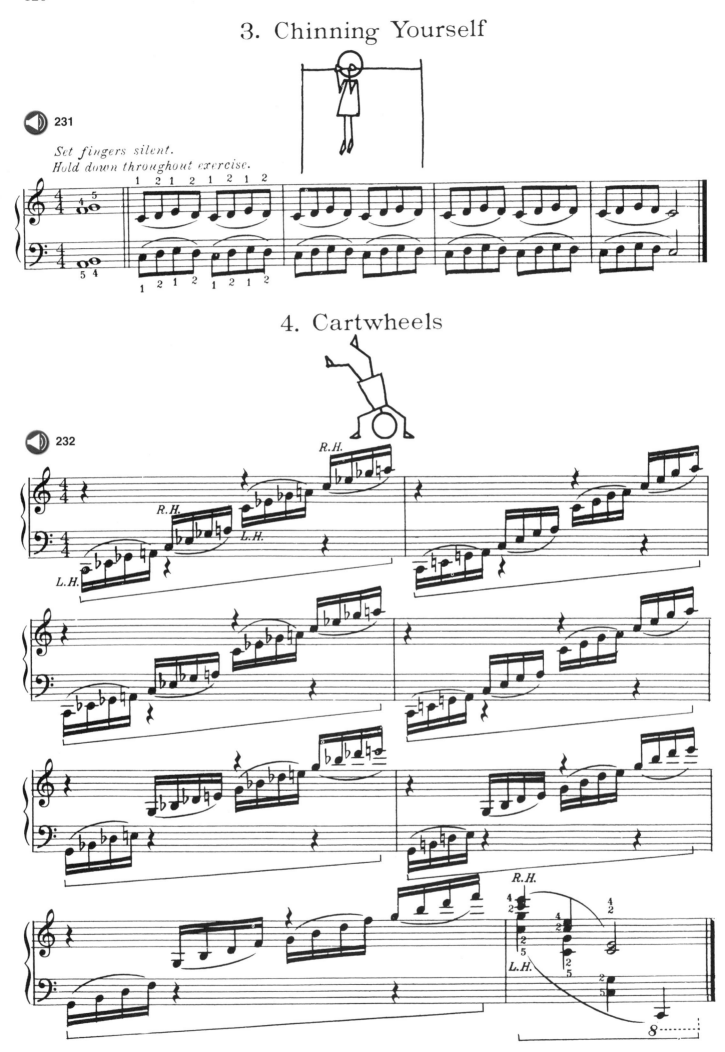

5. Bicycle Exercise

6. The Splits

7. Up and Down the Stairs

235

8. Running Down A Hill

236

Presto

Moderato

9. Deep Knee Bend

10. Leap Frog

11. Climbing

12. Fit as a Fiddle and Ready To Go

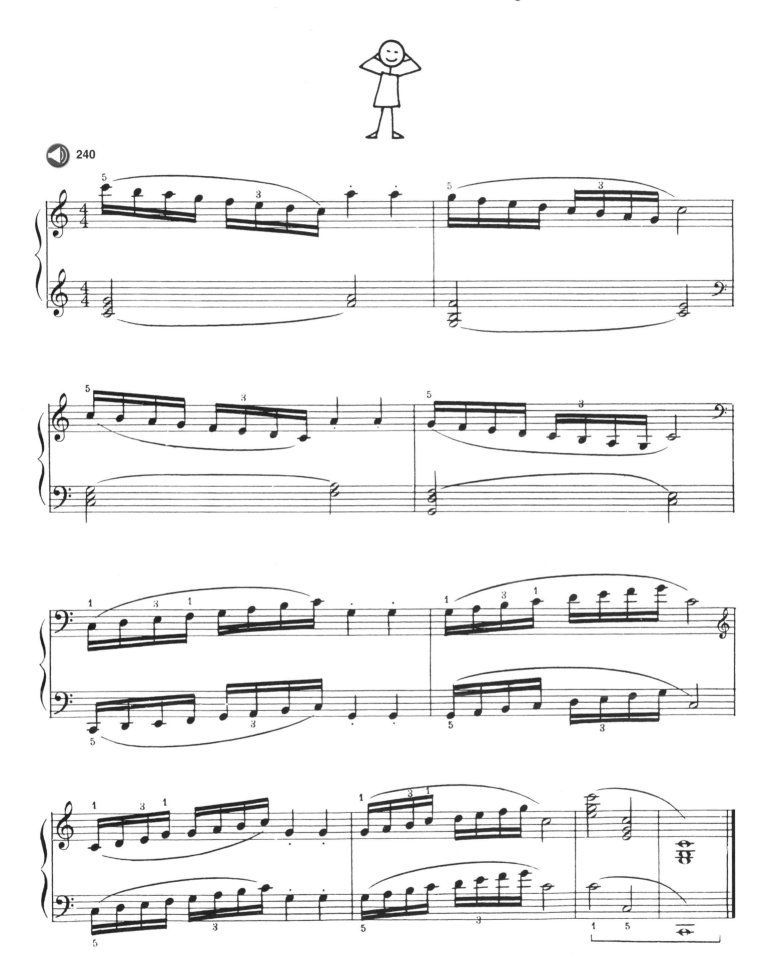

Edna Mae Burnam was a pioneer in piano publishing. The creator of the iconic *A Dozen a Day* technique series and *Step by Step* method was born on September 15, 1907 in Sacramento, California. She began lessons with her mother, a piano teacher who drove a horse and buggy daily through the Sutter Buttes mountain range to reach her students. In college Burnam decided that she too enjoyed teaching young children, and majored in elementary education at California State University (then Chico State College) with a minor in music. She spent several years teaching kindergarten in public schools before starting her own piano studio and raising daughters Pat and Peggy. She delighted in composing for her students, and took theory and harmony lessons from her husband David (a music professor and conductor of the Sacramento Symphony in the 1940s).

Burnam began submitting original pieces to publishers in the mid-1930s, and was thrilled when one of them, "The Clock That Stopped," was accepted, even though her remuneration was a mere $20. Undaunted, the industrious composer sent in the first *A Dozen a Day* manuscript to her Willis editor in 1950, complete with stick-figure sketches for each exercise. Her editor loved the simple genius of the playful artwork resembling a musical technique, and so did students and teachers: the book rapidly blossomed into a series of seven and continues to sell millions of copies. In 1959, the first book in the *Step by Step* series was published, with hundreds of individual songs and pieces along the way, often identified by whimsical titles in Burnam's trademark style.

The immense popularity of her books solidified Edna Mae Burnam's place and reputation in music publishing history, yet throughout her lifetime she remained humble and effervescent. "I always left our conversations feeling upbeat and happy," says Kevin Cranley, Willis president. "She could charm the legs off a piano bench," Bob Sylva of the *Sacramento Bee* wrote, "make a melody out of a soap bubble, and a song out of a moon beam."

Burnam died in 2007, a few months shy of her 100th birthday. "Music enriches anybody's life, even if you don't turn out to be musical," she said once in an interview. "I can't imagine being in a house without a piano."